PYTHON PROGRAMMING 101: STARTING WITH A VERSATILE LANGUAGE

Table of Contents

Chapter 1: Introduction

Chapter 2: Setting Up Your Python Environment

- Installation Guide: Windows, macOS, and Linux
- The Python Interpreter and IDLE
- Virtual Environments: Why and How?

Chapter 3: Basic Python Syntax

- Indentation and Whitespace
- Variables and Data Types
- Basic Operators

Chapter 4: Control Structures in Python

- Conditional Statements: If, Elif, and Else
- Loops: For and While
- Controlling Loop Execution: Break, Continue, and Pass

Chapter 5: Functions and Modules

- Defining and Calling Functions
- Parameters, Arguments, and Return Values
- Introduction to Python's Built-in Modules

Chapter 6: Data Structures in Python

- Lists and their Methods
- Tuples, Sets, and Dictionaries
- When to Use Which?

Chapter 7: Object-Oriented Programming (OOP) Basics

- What is OOP?
- Classes, Objects, and Attributes
- Methods and Inheritance

Chapter 8: Error Handling and Exceptions

CHAPTER 1: INTRODUCTION

Welcome to "Python Programming 101: Starting with a Versatile Language"! Whether you're a complete newcomer to programming or simply looking to pick up another tool for your coding repertoire, this guide is crafted for you. Our journey into the world of Python will be comprehensive yet easy to understand, ensuring that you leave with a firm grasp of the basics.

Why Choose Python?

Python, since its inception, has garnered global attention due to its simplicity and readability, making it a favorite among beginners and seasoned professionals alike. But it's not just the user-friendly syntax that makes Python so enticing; it's the sheer power and flexibility it brings to the table. With Python, one can script a simple task, build intricate web applications, analyze vast datasets, and even dabble in artificial intelligence and machine learning.

Many prominent tech giants, including Google, Spotify, and Netflix, employ Python for various tasks, further attesting to its robustness. Furthermore, with a thriving community behind it, there's a wealth of resources, tutorials, and libraries available, which means you'll rarely find yourself without support.

Overview of Python's Versatility

At its core, Python is a general-purpose language. This means it isn't confined to a single niche but rather can be applied across numerous domains. Web development, scientific computing, data analysis, artificial intelligence, automation, and more—Python has established its presence everywhere.

As we progress through this book, you'll come to appreciate the versatility firsthand. Each chapter is designed to introduce you to foundational concepts, bolstered with practical examples and exercises to solidify your understanding.

In the chapters ahead, we'll be setting up your Python environment, diving deep into its syntax, exploring data structures, understanding object-oriented programming, and much more. By the end, you'll have even developed your own Python application!

Get ready to embark on an enlightening journey into the world of Python programming. Whether your goal is personal growth, a career in software development, or just pure curiosity, Python is a worthy companion. And this guide, we hope, will be a catalyst for your success.

CHAPTER 2: SETTING UP YOUR PYTHON ENVIRONMENT

Starting with Python requires a conducive environment on your computer. This chapter will guide you step-by-step in setting up Python and ensuring you have the right tools to start coding. By the end, you'll be able to write, run, and experiment with Python scripts.

Installation Guide: Windows, macOS, and Linux

Windows:

1. Visit the official Python website at https://www.python.org/downloads/.
2. Download the latest version for Windows.
3. Run the installer. Make sure to check the box that

says "Add Python to PATH" before completing the installation. This ensures you can run Python from the Command Prompt.

4. Once installed, open the Command Prompt and type **python --version** to confirm the installation.

macOS:

1. Python 2.7 comes pre-installed on macOS, but we need Python 3.
2. Visit the official Python website to download the latest version for macOS.
3. Follow the installation instructions.
4. Once done, open the Terminal and type **python3 --version** to confirm the installation.

Linux:

1. Most Linux distributions come with Python pre-installed. Check by typing **python3 --version** in the terminal.
2. If not installed, you can use the package manager of your distribution to install Python. For example, on Ubuntu, you'd use **sudo apt-get install python3**.

The Python Interpreter and IDLE

Once Python is installed, you can use the Python interpreter to execute Python code directly. Simply open your terminal (or Command Prompt) and type **python** (or **python3** for macOS and Linux).

IDLE (Integrated Development and Learning Environment) is a basic editor that comes bundled with Python. It's useful for writing short scripts and quick testing. To launch IDLE, just type **idle** in your terminal or search for IDLE in your applications.

Virtual Environments: Why and How?

As you delve deeper into Python, you might work on multiple projects, each requiring different libraries and versions. Virtual environments allow you to create isolated spaces on your computer for Python projects, ensuring there's no clash between library versions.

To create a virtual environment:

1. Open your terminal and navigate to your project folder.

2. Type **python** **-m** **venv** **projectname_env** (Replace **projectname_env** with a name for your virtual environment).
3. To activate the environment, on Windows type **projectname_env\Scripts\activate**, and on macOS/Linux, use **source projectname_env/bin/activate**.

With the environment activated, any library you install using pip will only affect that environment, ensuring project consistency.

This chapter has set the foundation for your Python journey by ensuring you have the necessary tools and environment set up. As you advance, you'll appreciate the importance of these initial steps. In the next chapter, we'll dive into Python's syntax and start coding!

CHAPTER 3: BASIC PYTHON SYNTAX

Programming languages, much like spoken languages, have their grammar rules. These dictate how statements are structured and interpreted. In Python, this 'grammar' is referred to as syntax. In this chapter, we'll acquaint you with the fundamental syntax of Python, forming the base upon which more complex concepts will be built.

Indentation and Whitespace

Python's hallmark feature is its use of indentation to denote blocks of code. Unlike other languages that use braces { } for this purpose, Python relies on whitespace.

Consider this example:

if 5 > 3: print("Five is greater than three.")

The **print** statement is executed only if the condition **5 > 3** is **True**. Notice how the print statement is indented? That indentation signifies that it's part of the **if** block.

It's imperative to maintain consistent indentation throughout your code. Mixing spaces and tabs or altering indentation depth can lead to errors.

Variables and Data Types

Variables are used to store data values. In Python, unlike some other languages, you don't need to declare a variable before using it or declare its type. Python is dynamically-typed, meaning the type is determined at runtime.

Example:

name = "John" age = 30 is_student = True

Here, **name** is a string, **age** is an integer, and **is_student** is a boolean.

Python has several built-in data types:

- Text: **str** (e.g., **"Hello World"**)
- Numeric: **int** (e.g., **5**), **float** (e.g., **5.0**), **complex** (e.g., **5j**)
- Sequence: **list, tuple, range**
- Mapping: **dict**
- Set: **set, frozenset**
- Boolean: **bool** (e.g., **True, False**)
- Binary: **bytes, bytearray, memoryview**

Basic Operators

Operators are symbols that perform operations on variables and values. Python divides operators into several classes:

1. **Arithmetic Operators**: +, -, *, /, % (modulus), ** (exponentiation), // (floor division)
2. **Comparison Operators**: ==, !=, >, <, >=, <=
3. **Logical Operators**: and, or, not
4. **Assignment Operators**: =, +=, -=, *=, /=, etc.
5. **Bitwise Operators**: &, |, ^, ~, <<, >>

For example:

```
x = 5 y = 3 # Arithmetic Operations print(x + y) # Outputs: 8 #
Comparison Operations print(x > y) # Outputs: True
```

Python's syntax is intentionally designed to be clean and readable. This simplicity is what attracts many developers to the language. With the basics in place, you're ready to delve deeper and start controlling the flow of your Python programs, which we'll explore in the next chapter.

CHAPTER 4: CONTROL STRUCTURES IN PYTHON

Control structures allow developers to dictate the flow of execution in a program. With these structures in place, we can decide which code blocks to run based on certain conditions or repeatedly execute a block of code. This chapter will shed light on the primary control structures in Python: conditional statements and loops.

Conditional Statements: If, Elif, and Else

Python's conditional statements allow code to be executed if a certain condition is met.

```
temperature = 20 if temperature < 0: print("It's freezing!") elif
temperature < 10: print("It's cold.") else: print("It's warm.")
```

Here, only "It's warm." will be printed since the temperature is 20.

- The **if** keyword tests a condition. If the condition is **True**, the code under it runs.
- **elif** (short for 'else if') tests another condition if the previous one wasn't met.
- **else** captures any case where the preceding conditions aren't satisfied.

Loops: For and While

Loops are used to repeatedly execute a block of code.

1. **For Loop:** Used to iterate over a sequence (list, tuple, dictionary, string, or range).

```
fruits = ["apple", "banana", "cherry"] for fruit in fruits: print(fruit)
```

This prints:

apple banana cherry

2. **While Loop:** Executes a block of code as long as a condition remains true.

```
count = 1 while count <= 3: print(count) count += 1
```

This prints:

1 2 3

Controlling Loop Execution: Break, Continue, and Pass

Python provides control statements to influence the flow of loops:

- **break**: Exits the loop prematurely.

```
for num in [1, 2, 3, 4, 5]: if num == 4: break print(num)
```

Output:

1 2 3

- **continue:** Skips the current iteration and moves to the next one.

```
for num in [1, 2, 3, 4, 5]: if num == 4: continue print(num)
```

Output:

1 2 3 5

- **pass:** A null operation used as a placeholder when a statement is required syntactically but no action is needed.

```
for num in [1, 2, 3]: if num == 2: pass else: print(num)
```

Output:

```
Copy code
1 3
```

Control structures form the backbone of any programming language, empowering developers to craft logical and intricate flows in their software. As you become familiar with these constructs, you'll unlock the ability to handle more complex problems with ease. Up next, we delve into how to create reusable blocks of code with functions.

CHAPTER 5: FUNCTIONS AND MODULES

In programming, reusability is paramount. Functions allow us to encapsulate blocks of code into reusable units, leading to cleaner, more maintainable code. This chapter will provide an overview of defining and using functions, as well as a brief introduction to Python's built-in modules.

Defining and Calling Functions

A function is a block of organized, reusable code that performs a specific task. Functions provide modularity for your application and a high degree of code reusing.

Defining a function:

def greet(name): """This function greets the person passed in as a parameter.""" print(f"Hello, {name}.")

Calling a function:

greet("Alice")

Output:

Hello, Alice.

Note the triple quotes (""""). This is called a docstring and provides a brief description of the function's purpose.

Parameters, Arguments, and Return Values

In the context of functions:

- *Parameters* are the names listed in the function

definition.
- *Arguments* are the values sent to the function when it is called.

Functions can also send back results using the **return** statement:

```
def add(x, y): """This function returns the sum of two numbers."""
return x + y result = add(5, 3) print(result) # Outputs: 8
```

Introduction to Python's Built-in Modules

Python comes packed with a wide range of built-in modules, essentially files containing pre-written functions and variables, which provide essential functionality without requiring you to write additional code.

For instance, the **math** module provides mathematical functions:

import math # Finding the square root of 16 print(math.sqrt(16)) # Outputs: 4.0

To use a module, you must first **import** it. Once imported, you can use its functions by prefixing them with the module's name, as seen above.

Grasping the concept of functions is crucial to writing efficient Python code. With functions, you can structure your code into "chunks" that perform specific tasks, promoting readability and reusability. The next chapter will dive deeper into organizing data with Python's core data structures.

CHAPTER 6: DATA STRUCTURES IN PYTHON

Data structures allow us to organize and store data in our programs. Python offers built-in data structures that are flexible and easy to use. In this chapter, we will explore some of the most commonly used data structures: lists, tuples, sets, and dictionaries.

Lists and their Methods

A list is a collection that is ordered, changeable, and allows duplicate members.

Creating a list:

fruits = ["apple", "banana", "cherry"]

Accessing list items:

print(fruits[1]) # Outputs: banana

Adding and removing items:

fruits.append("orange") # Add to the end fruits.insert(1, "mango") # Insert at a specific index fruits.remove("banana") # Remove a specific item

Tuples, Sets, and Dictionaries

1. **Tuples:** Like a list, but unlike lists, once you create a tuple, you cannot alter its contents - similar to string data types.

```
fruit_tuple = ("apple", "banana", "cherry") print(fruit_tuple[0]) #
Outputs: apple
```

2. **Sets:** An unordered collection of unique items. They are useful when you want to ensure an element doesn't get repeated.

```
fruit_set = {"apple", "banana", "cherry"} fruit_set.add("mango") # Add
an item fruit_set.remove("banana") # Remove an item
```

3. **Dictionaries:** A collection of key-value pairs. Dictionaries are unordered, changeable, and do not allow duplicates.

```
fruit_colors = { "apple": "red", "banana": "yellow", "cherry": "red" }
print(fruit_colors["apple"]) # Outputs: red fruit_colors["apple"] =
"green" # Modify a value
```

When to Use Which?

- **Lists:** When you need an ordered collection of items that might have duplicates.
- **Tuples:** When you have an ordered collection of items that should not be modified.
- **Sets:** When you need to ensure each item is unique and order doesn't matter.
- **Dictionaries:** When you have a set of unique keys and associated values.

Understanding Python's core data structures is fundamental to effective programming. They help store, organize, and manipulate data efficiently. In our subsequent chapters, we will dive deeper into how to leverage the power of these structures for more complex operations.

CHAPTER 7:
OBJECT-ORIENTED PROGRAMMING (OOP) BASICS

Object-Oriented Programming (OOP) is a paradigm that provides a means to structure programs such that properties and behaviors are bundled into individual objects. Python, being a multi-paradigm language, supports OOP. This chapter will introduce the concepts of classes, objects, and inheritance, fundamental to OOP in Python.

What is OOP?

At its core, OOP revolves around the concept of objects, which are instances of classes. Imagine classes as blueprints: they define the attributes (data members) and behaviors (methods) that their objects will have. Objects are then instances of these classes.

For instance, if you have a class named **Car**, then a specific Toyota Corolla or a Honda Civic would be objects (instances) of this class.

Classes, Objects, and Attributes

Creating a class:

```
class Car: # A simple class attribute brand = "Unknown" # A special method called the initializer def __init__(self, model, color): self.model = model self.color = color
```

Instantiating objects:

```
car1 = Car("Corolla", "Blue") car2 = Car("Civic", "Red")
```

Accessing object attributes:

```
print(car1.model) # Outputs: Corolla print(car2.color) # Outputs: Red
```

Methods and Inheritance

Methods provide a way to add behaviors to classes. They are functions defined within a class.

```python
class Car: def __init__(self, brand, model): self.brand = brand
self.model = model def display_info(self): print(f"This is a {self.brand}
{self.model}.")
```

Using a method:

```python
car = Car("Toyota", "Corolla") car.display_info() # Outputs: This is a
Toyota Corolla.
```

Inheritance allows new classes (child classes) to take on the attributes and methods of existing classes (parent classes). This promotes code reuse and establishes a natural hierarchy between classes.

```python
class ElectricCar(Car): # ElectricCar inherits from Car def
__init__(self, brand, model, battery_size): super().__init__(brand,
model) # Call parent's initializer self.battery_size = battery_size
def battery_info(self): print(f"This car has a {self.battery_size} kWh
battery.")
```

Using inherited methods and attributes:

```python
tesla = ElectricCar("Tesla", "Model S", 100) tesla.display_info() #
Outputs: This is a Tesla Model S. tesla.battery_info() # Outputs: This
car has a 100 kWh battery.
```

Object-Oriented Programming encourages developers to see and model the real-world problems in terms of objects. The encapsulation, inheritance, and polymorphism provided by OOP can significantly improve code structure and reuse. In the next chapter, we'll delve into error handling, an essential aspect of building robust programs.

CHAPTER 8: ERROR HANDLING AND EXCEPTIONS

In any programming journey, encountering errors is inevitable. However, how a program responds to these errors can make the difference between a brief inconvenience and a critical failure. In this chapter, we'll explore how to gracefully handle errors in Python using exception handling mechanisms.

Common Python Errors for Beginners

1. **Syntax Errors:** Occurs when the Python parser detects a

mistake in your code's structure.

- Example: **print("Hello world"** (missing closing parenthesis)

2. **Name Errors:** Occur when a variable is used before it has been defined.
   - Example: **print(variable_name)** (assuming variable_name hasn't been defined)

3. **Type Errors:** Happen when an operation is applied to an inappropriate type.
   - Example: **"5" + 3** (Trying to add a string to an integer)

4. **Value Errors:** Raised when a function receives an argument of correct type but inappropriate value.
   - Example: **int("Hello")** (Trying to convert a word into an integer)

Try, Except, Else, and Finally

The primary mechanism for handling exceptions in Python is the **try...except** block.

```
try: result = 10 / 0 except ZeroDivisionError: print("You cannot divide
by zero!")
```

Output: **You cannot divide by zero!**

You can also handle multiple exceptions:

```
try: # Some code... except (TypeError, ValueError): # Handle the
exception
```

Or handle them separately:

```
try: # Some code... except TypeError: # Handle TypeError except
ValueError: # Handle ValueError
```

The **else** block can be used to specify a block of code to be executed
if no exceptions occur:

```
try: result = 10 / 5 except ZeroDivisionError: print("You cannot divide
by zero!") else: print("Division successful!")
```

Output: **Division successful!**

Finally, the **finally** block lets you specify actions that must be
executed regardless of whether an exception was raised:

```
try: result = 10 / 5 except ZeroDivisionError: print("You cannot divide
by zero!") finally: print("Executing the final block.")
```

Output:

Executing the final block.

Raising Exceptions

If you want to trigger exceptions in your code based on certain conditions, you can use the **raise** statement.

```
age = -1 if age < 0: raise ValueError("Age cannot be negative!")
```

This will raise a **ValueError** with the specified message.

Exception handling is crucial for building resilient programs. It ensures that unexpected errors don't crash the entire application and allows for graceful degradation of functionality. With the knowledge gained in this chapter, you can now write Python programs that robustly handle unforeseen issues.

CHAPTER 9: WORKING WITH FILES

Programs often need to interact with external files, whether it's for reading data, storing results, or managing configurations. Python offers straightforward mechanisms to deal with files, making file operations intuitive and efficient. This chapter delves into the basics of file handling in Python.

File I/O: Reading and Writing Text and Binary Files

1. Opening a File:

To work with a file, you first need to open it using the **open()** function:

```
file = open("example.txt", "r") # 'r' mode is for reading
```

Common modes include:

- **'r'**: Read (default)
- **'w'**: Write (Creates or truncates the file)
- **'a'**: Append (Creates the file if it doesn't exist)
- **'b'**: Binary mode

2. Reading from a File:

Once opened in read mode, you can retrieve the file's content:

```
content = file.read() # Reads the entire file lines = file.readlines() #
Reads the file line by line into a list
```

3. Writing to a File:

With the file opened in write or append mode, you can add content:

```
file = open("example.txt", "w") file.write("Hello, World!")
```

4. Closing a File:

After operations are done, it's essential to close the file:

file.close()

Using 'with' Statement for File Operations

The **with** statement simplifies exception handling by encapsulating common preparation and cleanup tasks in so-called context managers:

with open("example.txt", "r") as file: content = file.read() print(content) # File is automatically closed outside of the block

Organizing Files and Directories

Python's **os** module provides functions to interact with the operating system, including file and directory manipulation:

import os # Get the current working directory print(os.getcwd()) # List files and directories in the current directory print(os.listdir()) # Make a new directory os.mkdir("new_directory") # Rename a file or directory os.rename("old_name.txt", "new_name.txt") # Remove a file or directory os.remove("file_to_delete.txt") os.rmdir("directory_to_delete")

File handling forms the basis for many automation and data

processing tasks. Being proficient in reading from and writing to files allows you to harness the power of persistent storage in your applications. In the next segment, we will acquaint ourselves with essential libraries to extend Python's capabilities further.

CHAPTER 10: BASIC LIBRARIES TO KNOW

Python's extensive standard library is one of its greatest strengths, providing tools for various tasks right out of the box. However, the Python ecosystem is vast, enriched by numerous third-party packages that cater to niche requirements. In this chapter, we'll touch upon three foundational libraries that extend Python's capabilities in the realms of numerical operations, data manipulation, and visualization.

1. NumPy for Numerical Operations

NumPy (Numerical Python) is a library for handling arrays (especially numerical data), offering mathematical functions to operate on these arrays more efficiently than Python's built-in tools.

```
import numpy as np # Creating an array arr = np.array([1, 2, 3, 4, 5]) #
Basic operations print(arr + 10) # Adds 10 to each element: [11 12 13
14 15]
```

NumPy's power shines in its functionality for linear algebra, statistical operations, and other mathematical tools.

2. Pandas for Data Manipulation

Pandas offers data structures and operations for efficiently manipulating large datasets. Its primary structures, Series and DataFrame, handle a wide variety of tasks.

```
import pandas as pd # Creating a DataFrame data = { 'Name': ['Alice',
'Bob', 'Charlie'], 'Age': [25, 30, 35], 'City': ['New York', 'San Francisco',
'Los Angeles'] } df = pd.DataFrame(data) # Basic DataFrame operations
print(df.head()) # Displays the first 5 rows print(df[df['Age'] > 30]) #
Filtering rows based on a condition
```

Pandas integrates well with other libraries, making data import, manipulation, and export a breeze.

3. Matplotlib for Data Visualization

Matplotlib is a plotting library that produces static, animated, and interactive visualizations in Python. It's particularly useful for visualizing complex data in an easy-to-understand format.

```
import matplotlib.pyplot as plt # Basic line plot x = [1, 2, 3, 4, 5]
y = [2, 4, 6, 8, 10] plt.plot(x, y) plt.xlabel('X-axis') plt.ylabel('Y-axis')
```

plt.title('Simple Line Plot') plt.show()

While Matplotlib offers a wide range of plotting functions, its syntax and structure serve as a foundation for other visualization libraries in Python.

These three libraries only scratch the surface of Python's expansive ecosystem. However, they represent crucial tools that any budding Pythonista should familiarize themselves with, given their ubiquity in data-related tasks. In our upcoming chapter, we'll guide you through a capstone project, encapsulating the concepts learned so far.

CHAPTER 11: FINAL PROJECT: BUILDING A SIMPLE PYTHON APPLICATION

After journeying through Python's core concepts, it's time to put our knowledge into practice. In this capstone project, we'll create a simple contact book application that allows users to add, view, update, and delete contacts.

Project Overview

Our contact book will store the following details:

1. Full Name
2. Phone Number
3. Email Address

Step-by-Step Implementation Guide

1. Setting up the Data Structure:

We'll use a list of dictionaries to store our contacts.

```python
pythonCopy code
contacts = []
```

2. Adding a New Contact:

Define a function to add contacts.

```python
def add_contact(): name = input("Enter full name: ") phone = input("Enter phone number: ") email = input("Enter email address: ") contact = {"name": name, "phone": phone, "email": email} contacts.append(contact) print(f"Added {name} to contacts.")
```

3. Displaying All Contacts:

```python
def display_contacts(): for contact in contacts: print(f"Name: {contact['name']}, Phone: {contact['phone']}, Email: {contact['email']}")
```

4. Updating an Existing Contact:

```python
def update_contact(name): for contact in contacts: if contact['name'] == name: contact['phone'] = input("Enter new phone number: ")
```

```
contact['email'] = input("Enter new email address: ") print(f"Updated
details for {name}.") return print(f"No contact found with the name
{name}.")
```

5. Deleting a Contact:

```
def delete_contact(name): global contacts contacts = [contact for
contact in contacts if contact['name'] != name] print(f"Deleted {name}
from contacts.")
```

6. User Interface:

Construct a simple CLI (Command-Line Interface) loop to interact
with users.

```
while True: print("\n--- Contact Book ---") print("1. Add Contact")
print("2. View Contacts") print("3. Update Contact") print("4. Delete
Contact") print("5. Exit") choice = input("Enter your choice: ") if
choice == "1": add_contact() elif choice == "2": display_contacts()
elif choice == "3": name_to_update = input("Enter the name of the
contact to update: ") update_contact(name_to_update) elif choice ==
"4": name_to_delete = input("Enter the name of the contact to delete:
") delete_contact(name_to_delete) elif choice == "5": print("Goodbye!")
break else: print("Invalid choice. Please try again.")
```

Testing and Debugging Your Application

Now that our application is ready, run the program and try out all functionalities. Ensure each function works as expected and handle any edge cases or errors that might arise.

With the completion of this project, you've successfully applied many of the concepts learned throughout this eBook. This exercise should cement your foundational understanding of Python and prepare you for more advanced projects and learning.

CHAPTER 12: CONCLUSION AND NEXT STEPS

Congratulations on reaching the end of "Python Programming 101: Starting with a Versatile Language"! Over the course of this eBook, we've journeyed from the absolute basics of setting up Python to building a functional application. Along the way, we delved deep into Python's core concepts, syntax, data structures, object-oriented programming, and more.

Recap

Here's a brief overview of what we've covered:

1. **Introduction to Python:** The reasons behind Python's popularity and where it stands in today's tech landscape.

2. **Python Basics:** Setting up the environment, understanding syntax, and diving into foundational concepts.
3. **Data Structures:** From simple data types to more complex structures like lists, dictionaries, and sets.
4. **OOP in Python:** Creating classes, objects, and leveraging inheritance for modular code.
5. **File Handling and Libraries:** Reading/writing files and exploring essential libraries like NumPy, Pandas, and Matplotlib.
6. **Building a Python Application:** Combining our knowledge to craft a simple contact book application.

Where to Go from Here

The world of Python is vast and filled with opportunities. Here are some recommendations to expand your Python prowess:

1. **Dive Deeper into Libraries:** Libraries like TensorFlow and PyTorch for Machine Learning, Flask and Django for web development, and many others offer specialized tools for various domains.
2. **Algorithm and Data Structures:** Enhance your problem-solving skills. Websites like LeetCode, CodeWars, and HackerRank offer countless challenges.
3. **Join the Community:** Engage with other learners and professionals. Platforms like Stack Overflow, Python forums, and local Python meet-ups can be invaluable.
4. **Collaborate on Projects:** Use platforms like GitHub to collaborate with others, contribute to open-source projects, or start your own.
5. **Continuous Learning:** Technologies evolve. Stay

updated with the latest in Python and associated frameworks through courses, workshops, and webinars.

Final Words

Python is a versatile and powerful language, but it's just a tool. Your creativity, problem-solving skills, and perseverance will determine what you can achieve with it. Embrace the challenges, learn from mistakes, and always keep the end goal in mind.

Remember, the journey of mastering Python—or any language—is ongoing. With passion and dedication, there's no limit to what you can achieve. Happy coding!

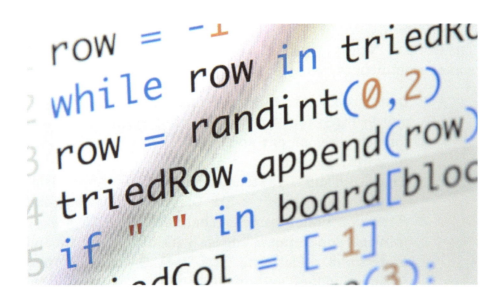

www.ingramcontent.com/pod-product-compliance
Lightning Source LLC
LaVergne TN
LVHW072050060326
832903LV00053B/318